A Proust Questionnaire

tarcherperigee

An imprint of Penguin Random House LLC
375 Hudson Street
New York, New York 10014

Library of Congress Cataloging-in-Publication Data

Names: Neborsky, Joanna, author.
Title: A Proust questionnaire : discover your truest self—in 30 simple questions / Joanna Neborsky.
Description: New York, NY : TarcherPerigee, [2016]
Identifiers: LCCN 2016015606 | ISBN 9781101983027 (pbk.)
Subjects: LCSH: Personality—Miscellanea. | Conduct of life—Miscellanea. | Proust, Marcel, 1871-1922.
Classification: LCC BF698.3 .N43 2016 | DDC 155.2/83—dc23

Printed in the United States of America
1 3 5 7 9 10 8 6 4 2

Book design by Joanna Neborsky

A Proust Questionnaire

Discover Your Truest Self—in 30 Simple Questions

Joanna Neborsky

A TarcherPerigee Book

AN
ALBUM
CONFESSIONS
RECORD
FEELINGS
&c

Introduction

Good news! It's all about ~~me~~ YOU! .

Sure, it's possible, in a world of insta-face-vine, to invent and perform you, or someone proximate, for a large audience. But look, here is a smaller, more intimate canvas: 120 pages, mostly white, with a few smudges (sorry), where you can try on thirty or so classic interview questions, which have come down to us in one form or another as the Proust Questionnaire. This confessional seeks to reveal your most secret, least-clothed self through a series of q's all about your loves, wants, fears, and, let's face it, bizarre tastes. The results are just for you, or for you and others if you trust them (*which I would not!*). No user agreement is limiting you to 140 characters, or even to words themselves. Cross-hatch your responses. Uncork the glitter gun. RE-CORK THE GLITTER GUN. Have a proportionate amount of fun.

Another thing. We do not mean to disappoint the lit majors (any more than usual), but if you have not yet read the collective four thousand pages of Marcel Proust's *In Search of Lost Time*, do not consider the Proust Questionnaire a proper introduction to his work. Proust didn't write it. ⇨ Scandale!

In 1886, young Antoinette Faure asked her fifteen-year-old friend Marcel (seated, a bit younger, on the preceding spread) to fill out an entry in a red-leather book inscribed *Confessions. An Album to Record Thoughts, Feelings, etc*. The confession album, full of the sort of gently philosophic inquiries that we have repeated, with some affectionate twists, in this book, was a literary invention of the Victorians, a mechanism for young English women and men (but mostly women) to swap intimacies and deepen bonds of friendship. The fad spread; Marcel obliged Antoinette. His responses betray a wild precocity (what other teen might admit to most wanting to live "in the country of the ideal"?) and some reticence (four questions, blank). A few years later, Marcel tried another round of the parlor game. This one revealed a more classically lovelorn Proust (now he'd like to live "where feelings of tenderness would always be reciprocate"), and was published during his lifetime as "Salon Confessions."

The critic Evan Kindley guesses that Proust "would have despised the phenomenon" of the personality quiz that bears his name. In the century and a half since Marcel first scrawled dreamily into Antoinette's diary, the questionnaire has become a commonplace of the celebrity interview in Europe and North America—not only a rite of prestige, but a factory of minute revelations and bon mots. We who are not Proust can be grateful for its endurance, however. First, it is how we know that Kiefer Sutherland's favorite word is "gravitas." Second, it is how I know you are about to have a splendid afternoon of picturesque mulling, doodled wisdoms, and—to quote the album of 1886 that started it all—"*etc.*"

Ready, then?

Your turn.

Impress us, ___________!

Spill.

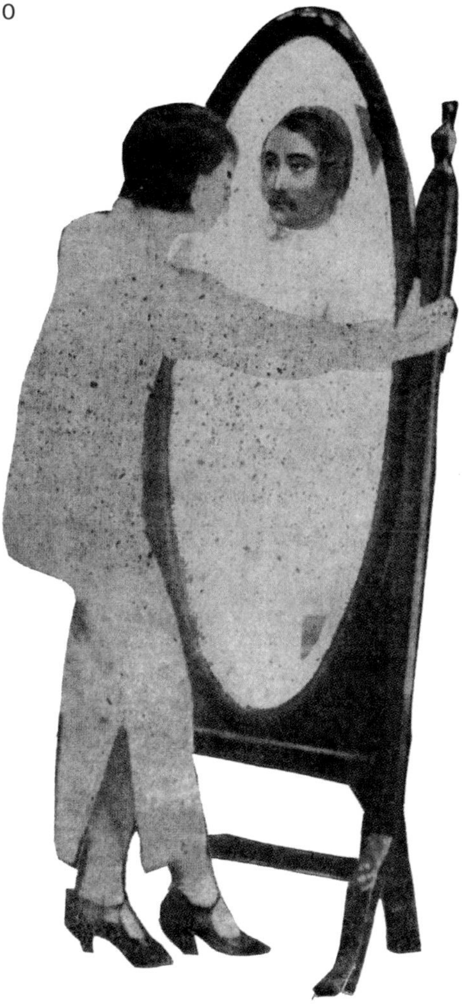

"**Who are we, Bob?**"

a method of personality analysis

1.

Where to begin?

What is your greatest fear?

Pardon our outburst. We glimpsed a limitless void.

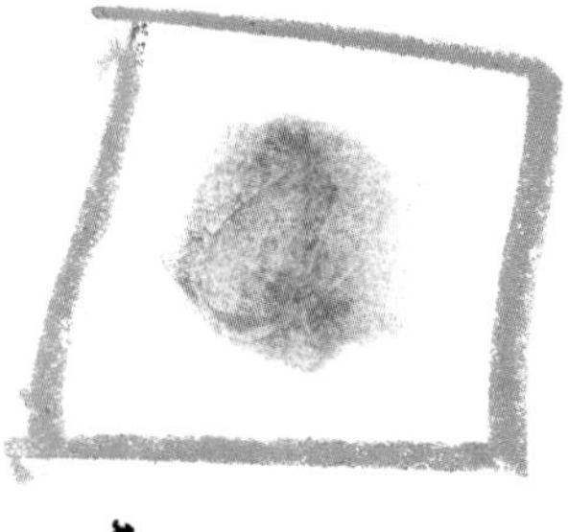

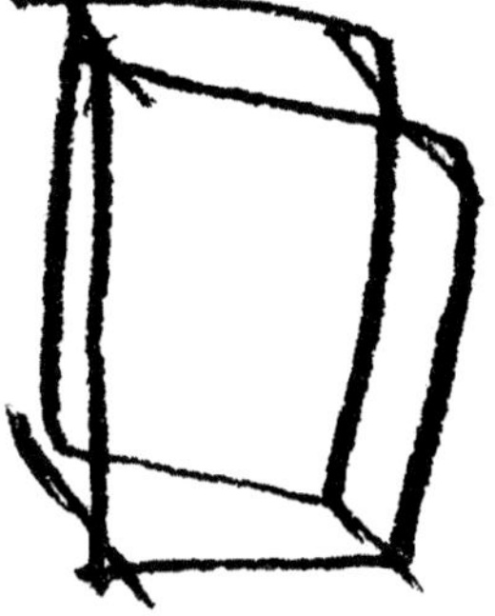

2

99
95
90
80
70
60
50
40
30
20
10
5
1

What do you consider the <u>lowest</u> depth of misery?

And why?

3.

What is your favorite way of spending time?

And why?

Schedule your perfect day.

4.

With which historical figures do you most identify?

PLEASE EXPLAIN.

5.

When and where were you happiest?

Discuss.

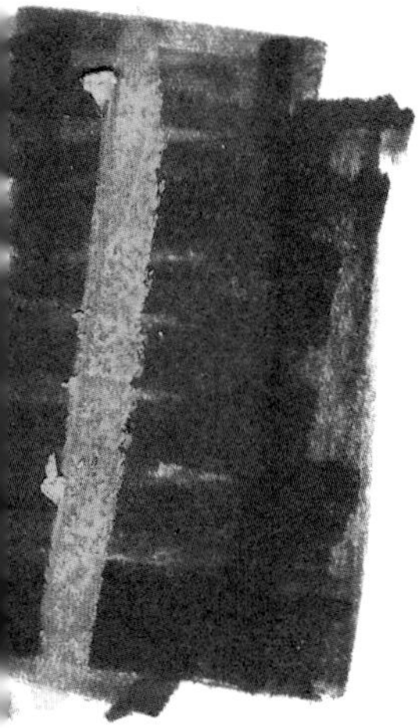

What is your current STATE of mind?

6

TELL US ALL ABOUT IT.

7.

What is your greatest achievement?

What qualities of your friends do you most admire?

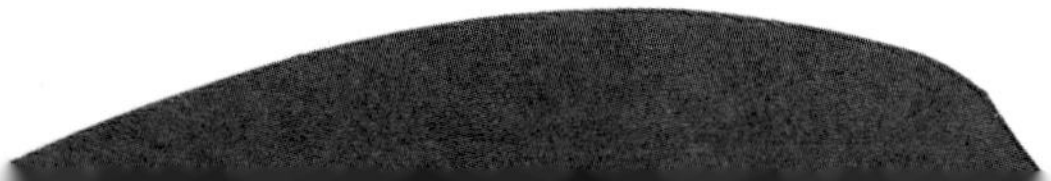

8.

9
BEE GEES
·boogie child·
PET

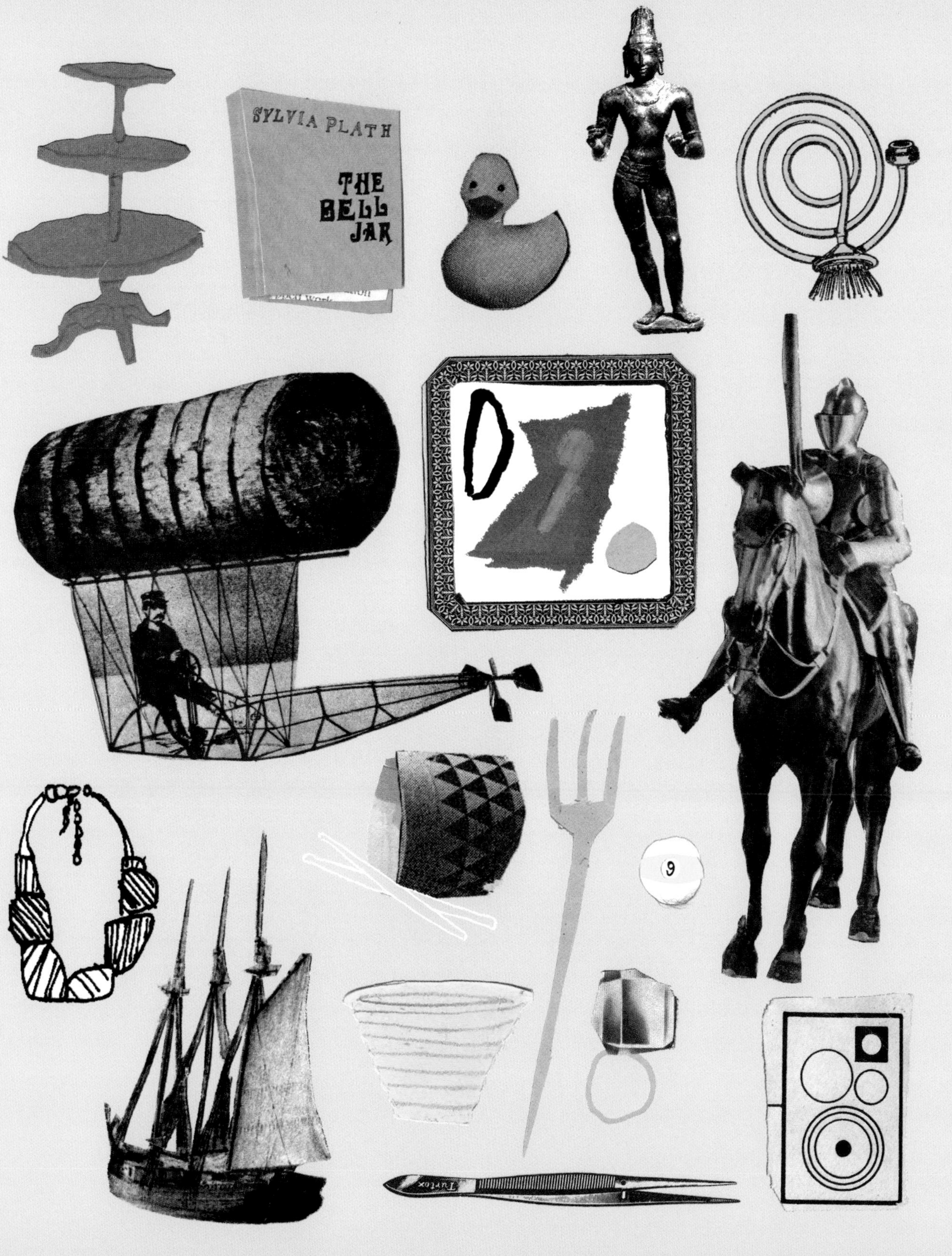
SYLVIA PLATH
THE BELL JAR
9
Turtox

What physical possession do you treasure the most?

PLEASE EXPLAIN.

If you'd like, place it in this vitrine.

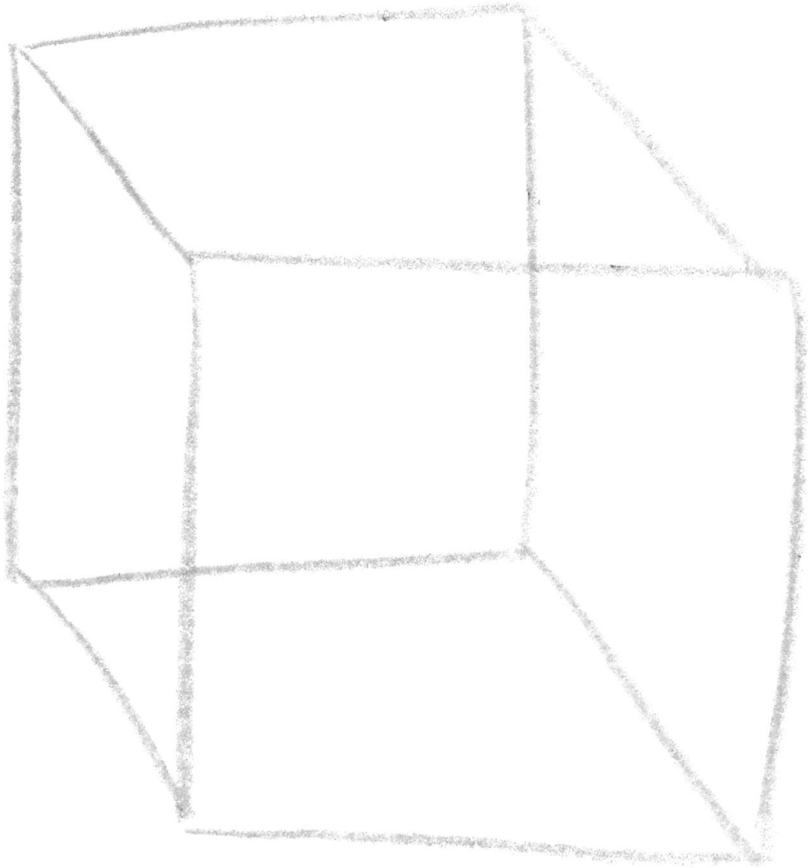

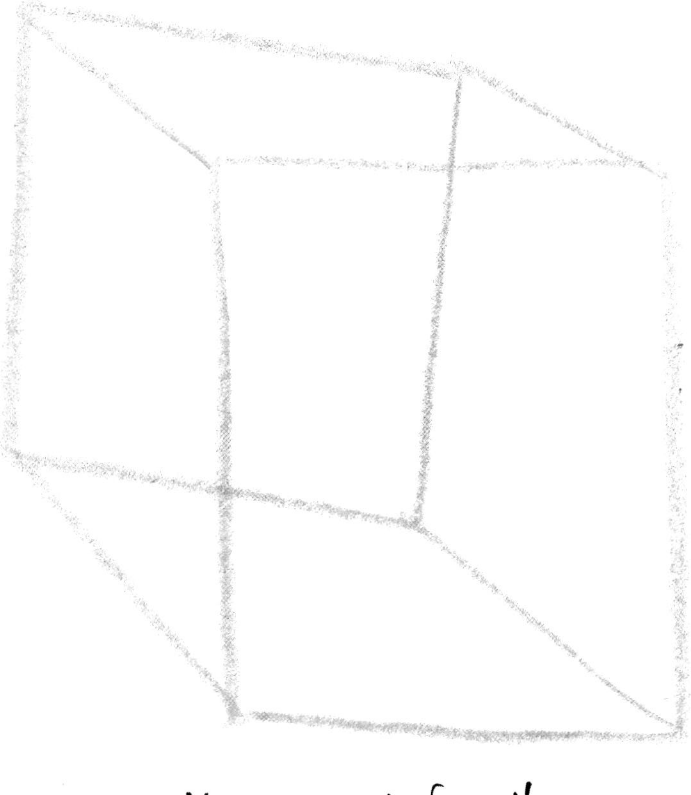

Your second-favorite can go
in this smaller vitrine.

*

Firs soldiers carrying clubs; these were all shap three gardeners, oblong and flat, with their hands and feet at the corners: next the ten courtiers: these were ornamented all over with diamonds, and walked two and two, as the soldiers did. After these came the royal children; there were ten of them, and the little dears came jumping merrily along hand in hand, in couples: they were all ornamented with hearts. Next came the guests, mostly Kings and Queens, and among them Alice recognised the White Rabbit: it was talking in a hurried nervous manner, smiling at everything that was said, and went by without noticing her. Then followed the Knave of Hearts, carrying the King's crown on a crimson velvet cushion; and, last of all this grand procession, came THE KING AND QUEEN OF HEARTS.

Who are your favorite heroes in fiction?

And why?

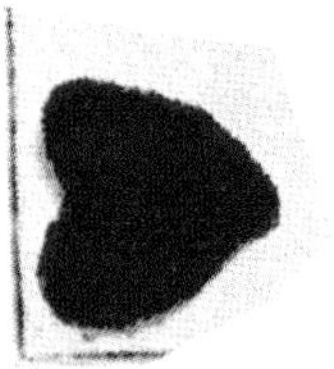

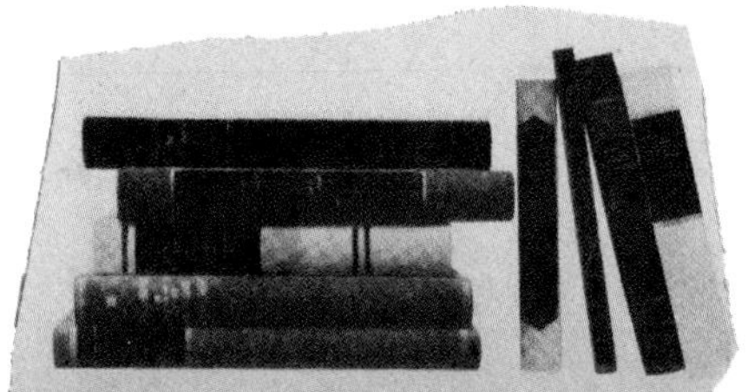

Quote them here:

11

SUGGESTIONS

What would be the one thing

you would change about yourself?

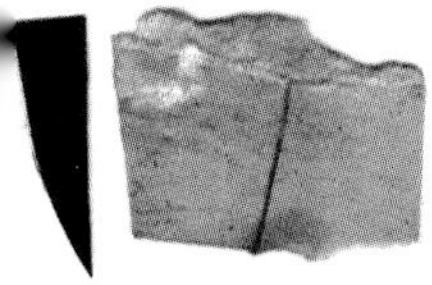

If you're stumped, please refer to the suggestion box we've been passing around since the introduction.

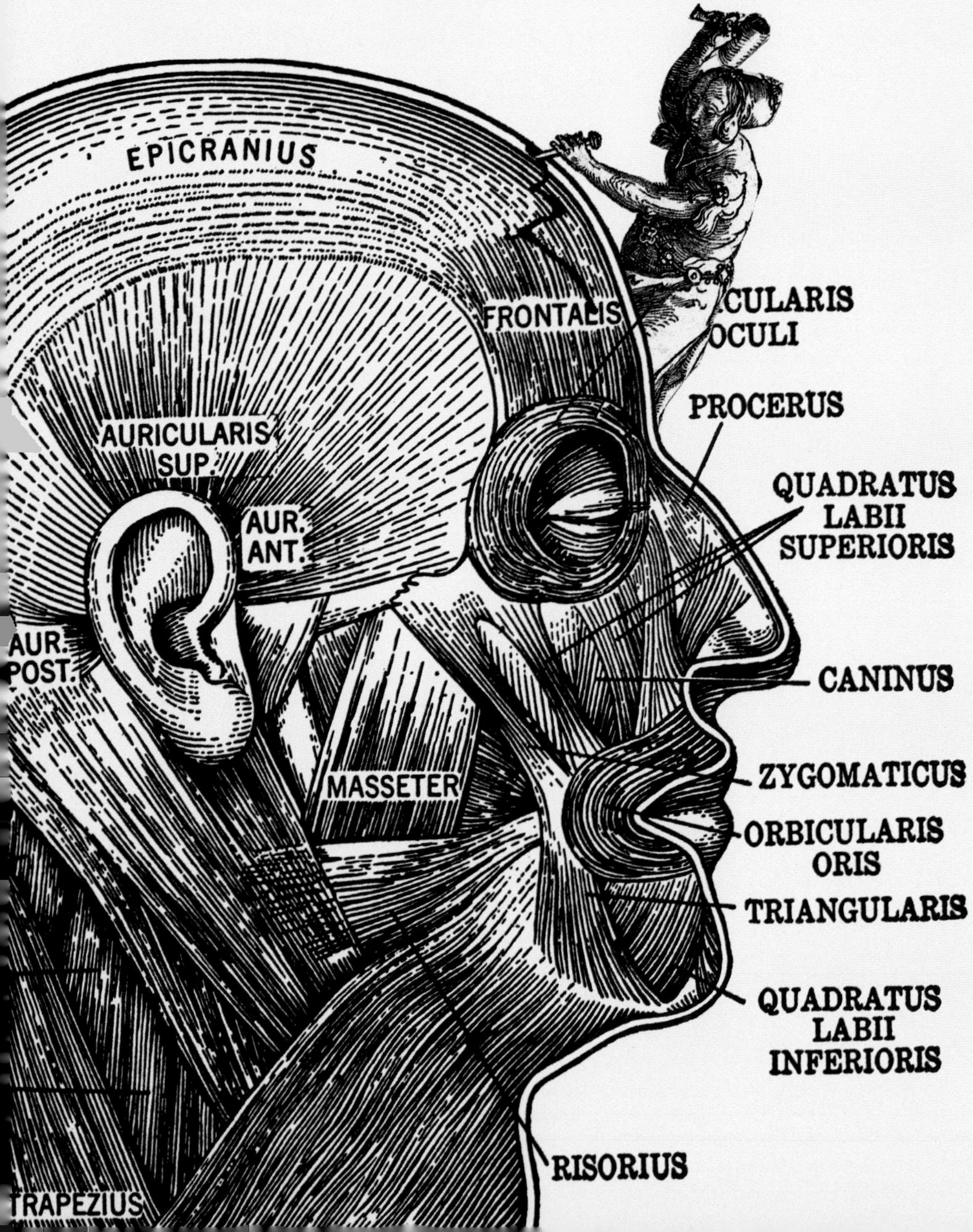
EPICRANIUS
FRONTALIS
CULARIS
OCULI
PROCERUS
AURICULARIS
SUP.
AUR.
ANT.
QUADRATUS
LABII
SUPERIORIS
AUR.
POST.
CANINUS
MASSETER
ZYGOMATICUS
ORBICULARIS
ORIS
TRIANGULARIS
QUADRATUS
LABII
INFERIORIS
RISORIUS
TRAPEZIUS

12.

What quality do you most deplore in yourself?

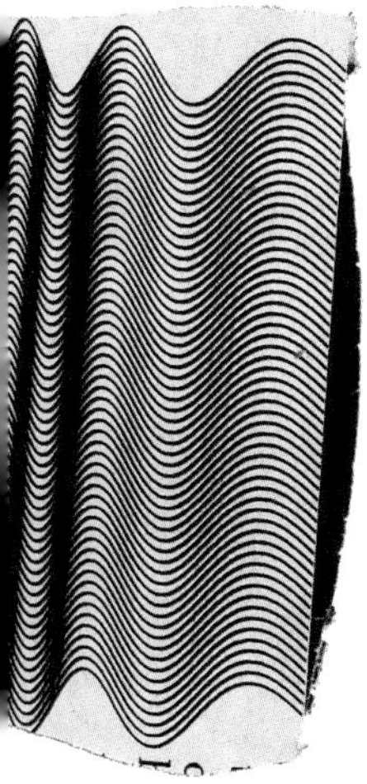

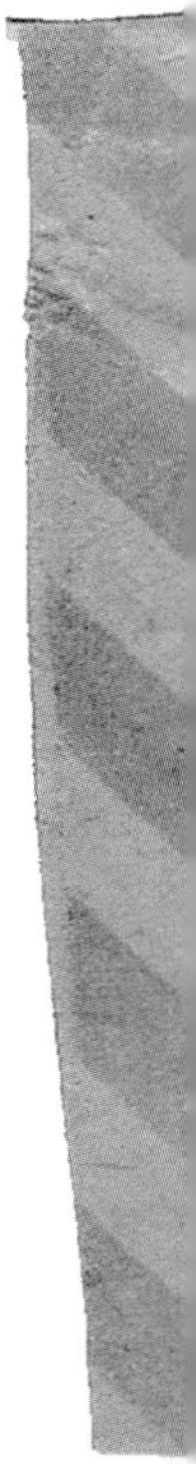

13

Now, what quality do you most deplore in others?

Rail wildly in the "rail wildly" box.

14.

card!

That's weird — I *knew* you were about to tell me about your greatest extravagance.

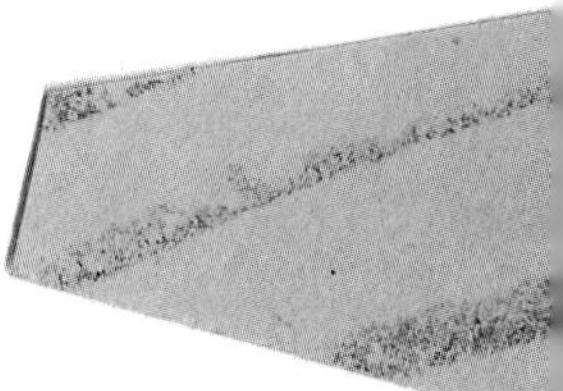

vroom

15

What is your favorite journey?

And why?

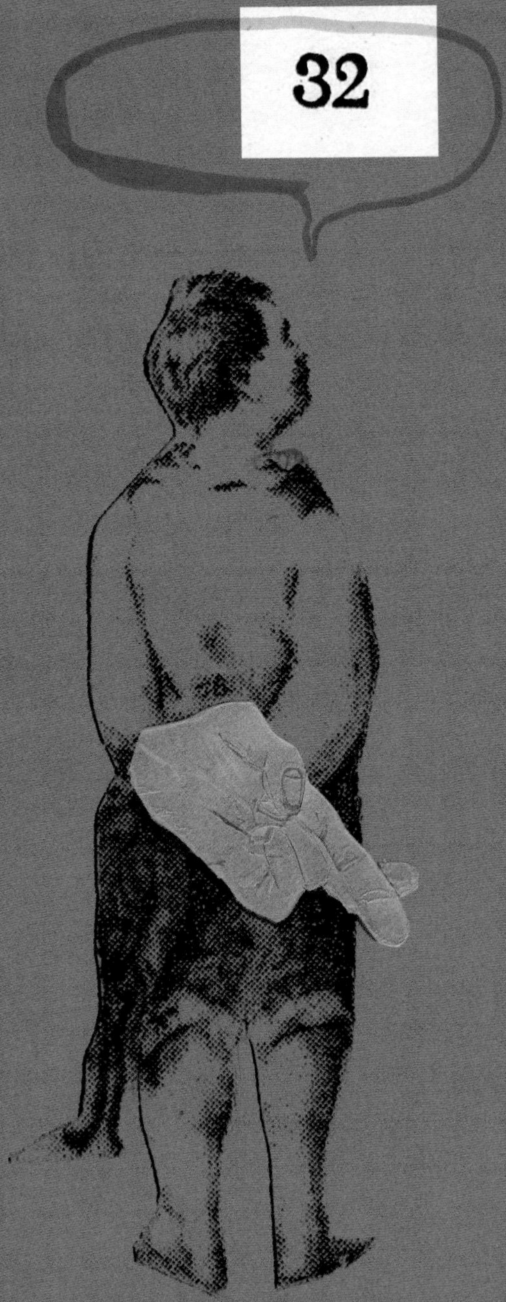
32

On what occasion do you lie? **DISCUSS.**

17. FACE LIFTING BY EXERCISE

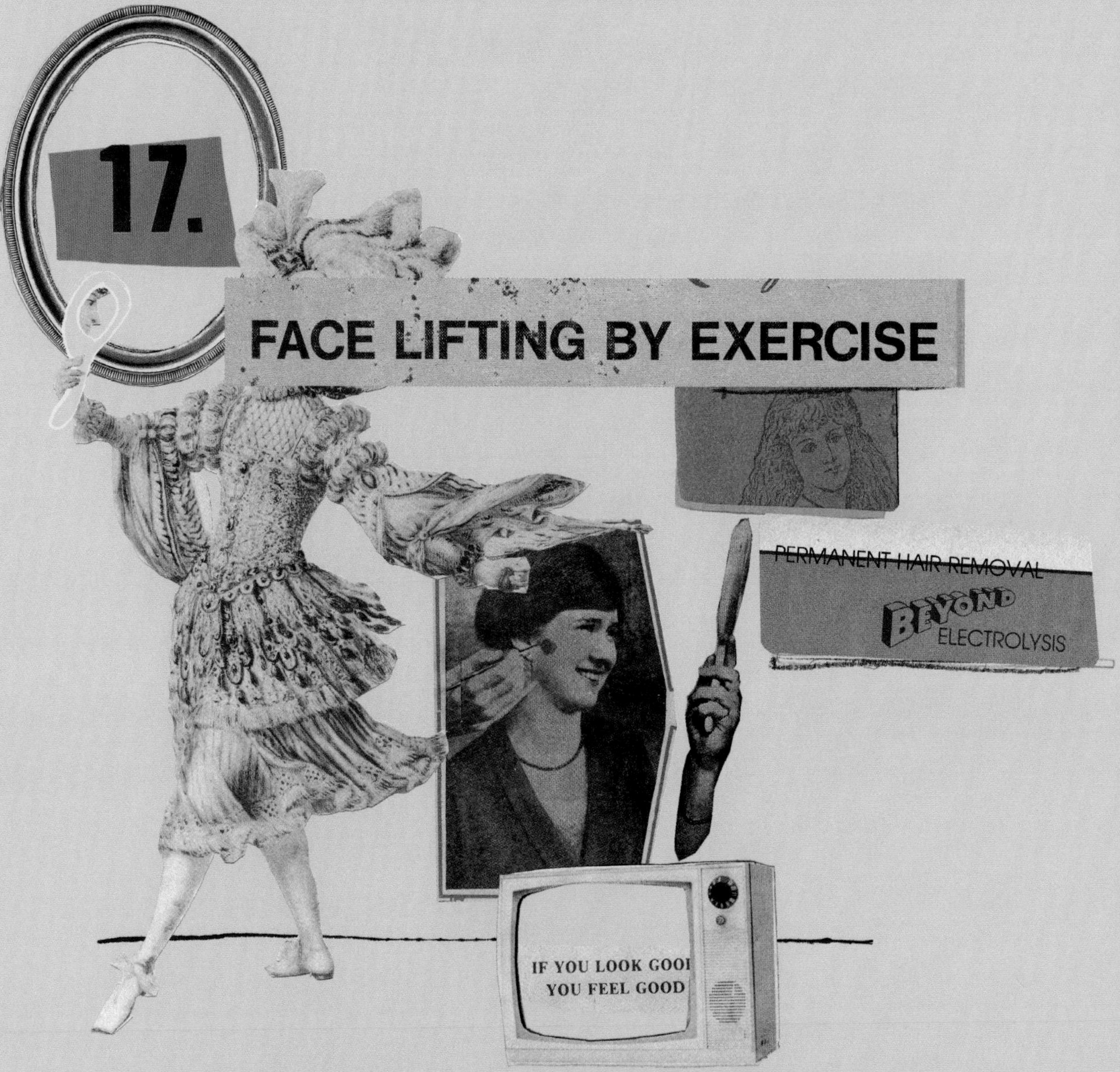
PERMANENT HAIR REMOVAL
BEYOND
ELECTROLYSIS
IF YOU LOOK GOOI
YOU FEEL GOOD

What do you dislike the most about your appearance?

PLEASE EXPLAIN.

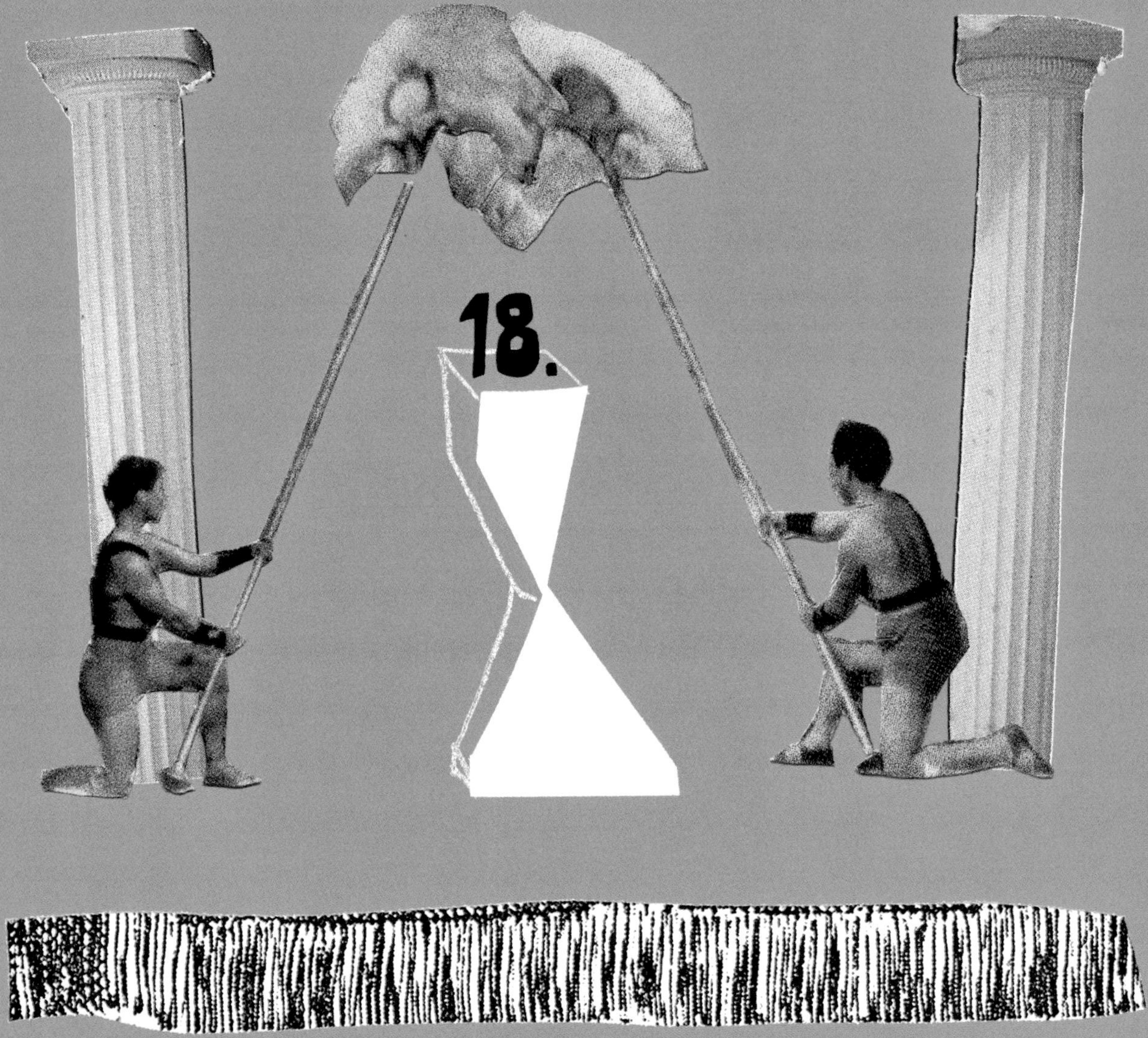
18.

the most overrated virtue?

What do you consider the most overrated virtue?

Discuss.

19.

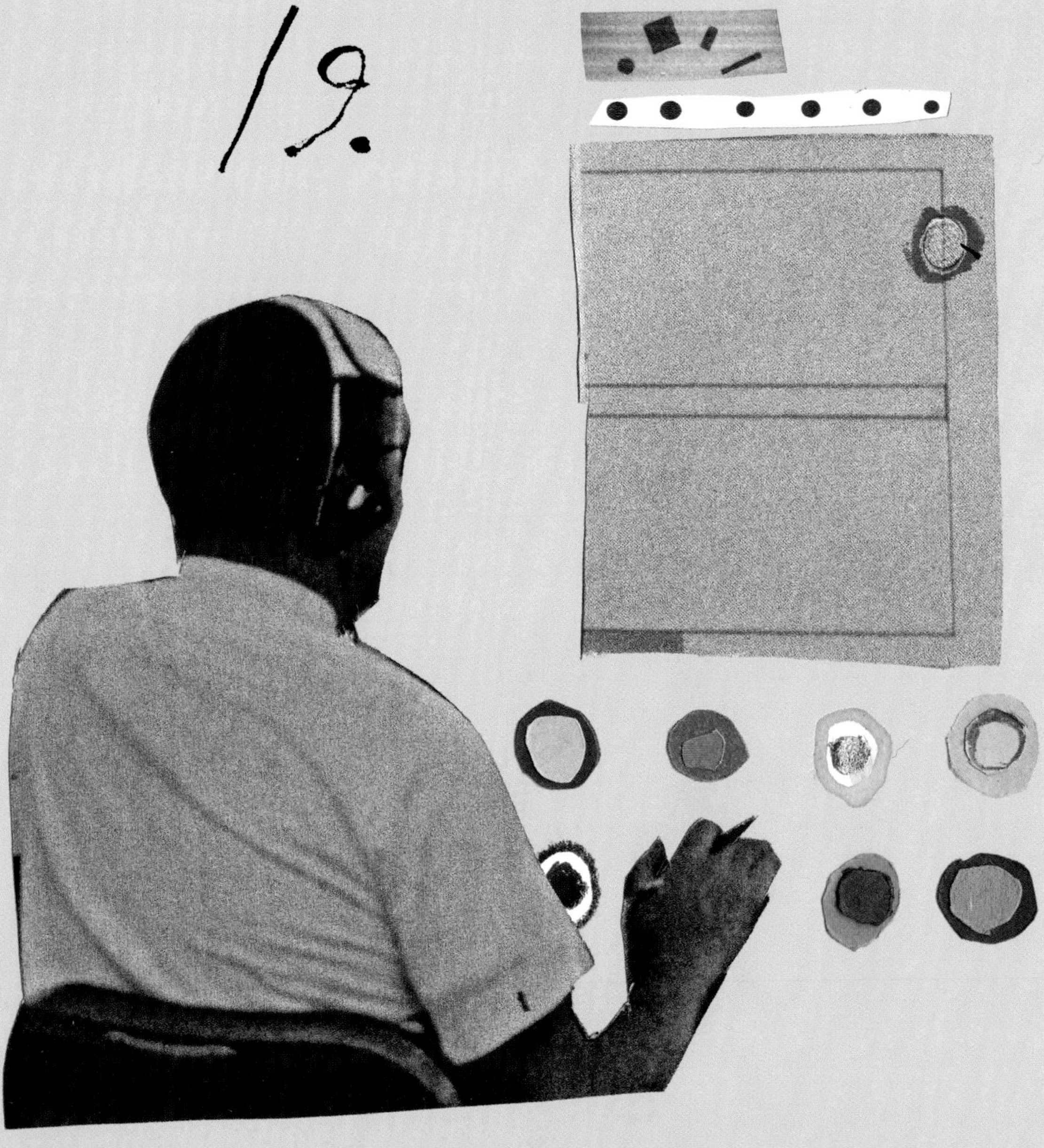

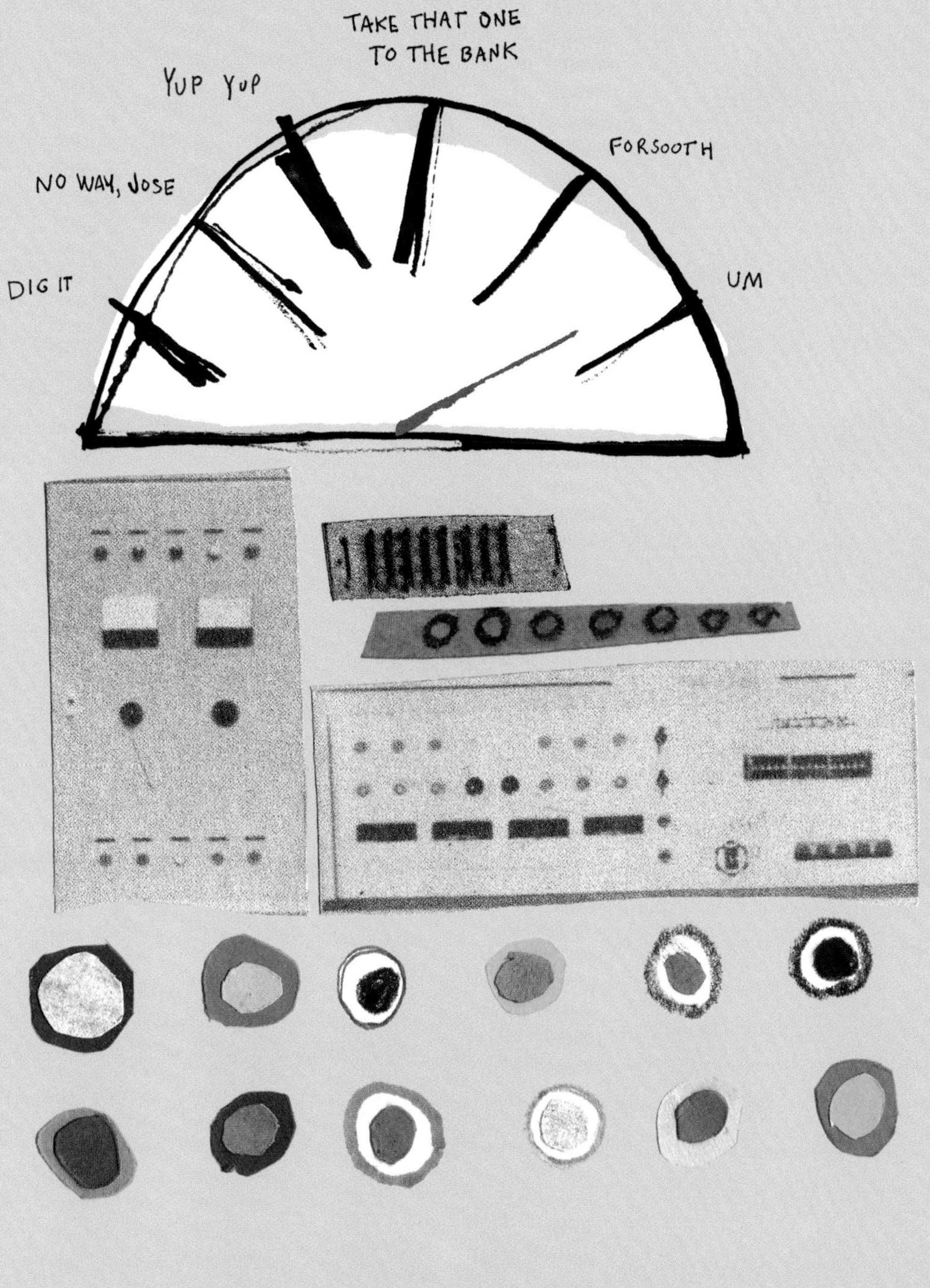
TAKE THAT ONE
TO THE BANK
YUP YUP
FORSOOTH
NO WAY, JOSE
DIG IT
UM

Which words or phrases do you most overuse, chief?

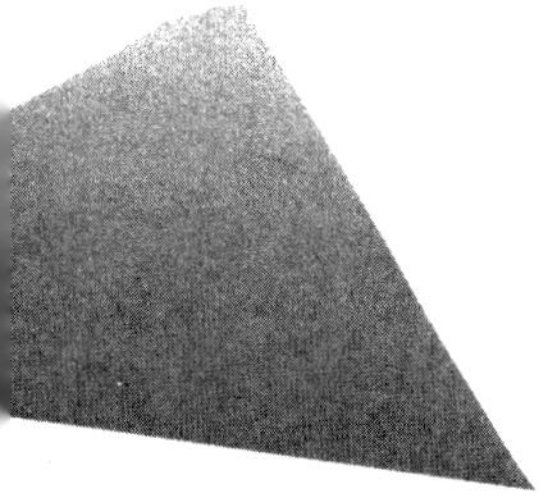

20.

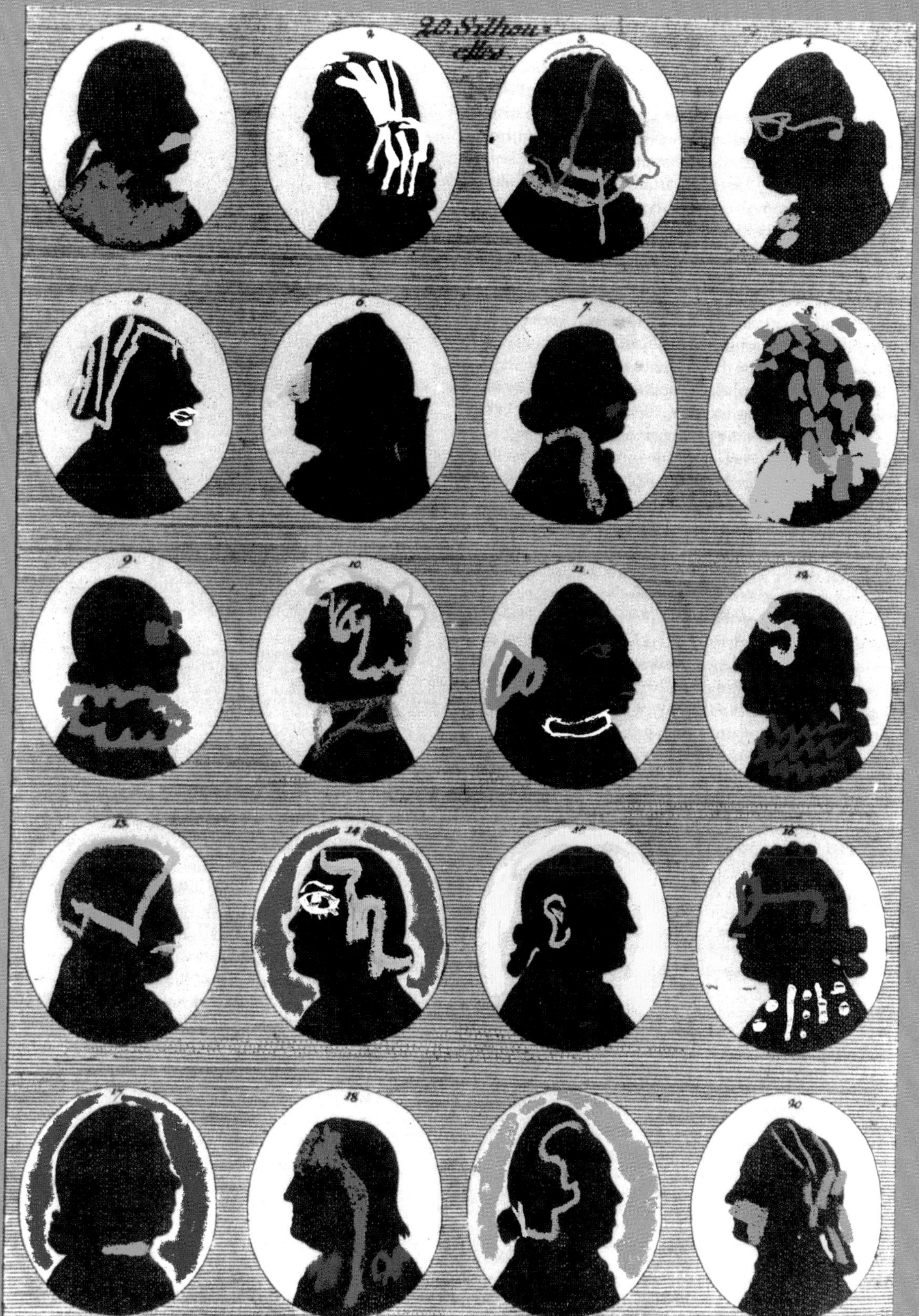
20. Silhou-
ettes.

What is your most marked characteristic?

PLEASE EXPLAIN.

21.000000 km

If you had one place in which
to spend the rest of your life,
where would it be?

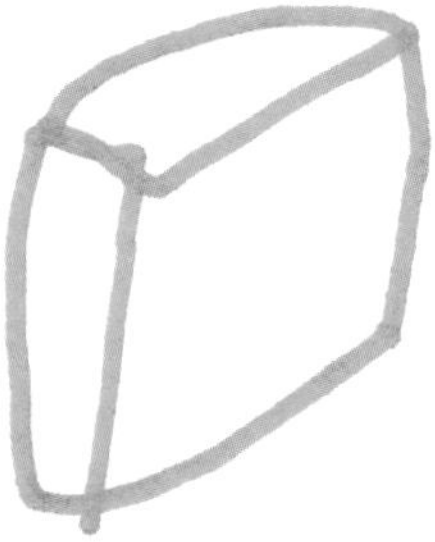

This question sponsored by South Florida.

22.

If you were to die and come back as a person or animal, who or what would you be?

TELL US ALL ABOUT IT.

Who has influenced you more than any other person?

And why?

TOO BLESSED
TO BE
STRESSED
24.

keep your friends close

What is your personal motto?

Now, emblazon it on a coat of arms.

25.

Who are your real-life heroes?

Your real-life heroes:

Personality, we know, does not develop in a vacuum, but through the movement, feeling, and thinking of a specific body.

A Sonnet

26.

What is the talent you would most like to have?

DISCUSS.

We're getting near the end.

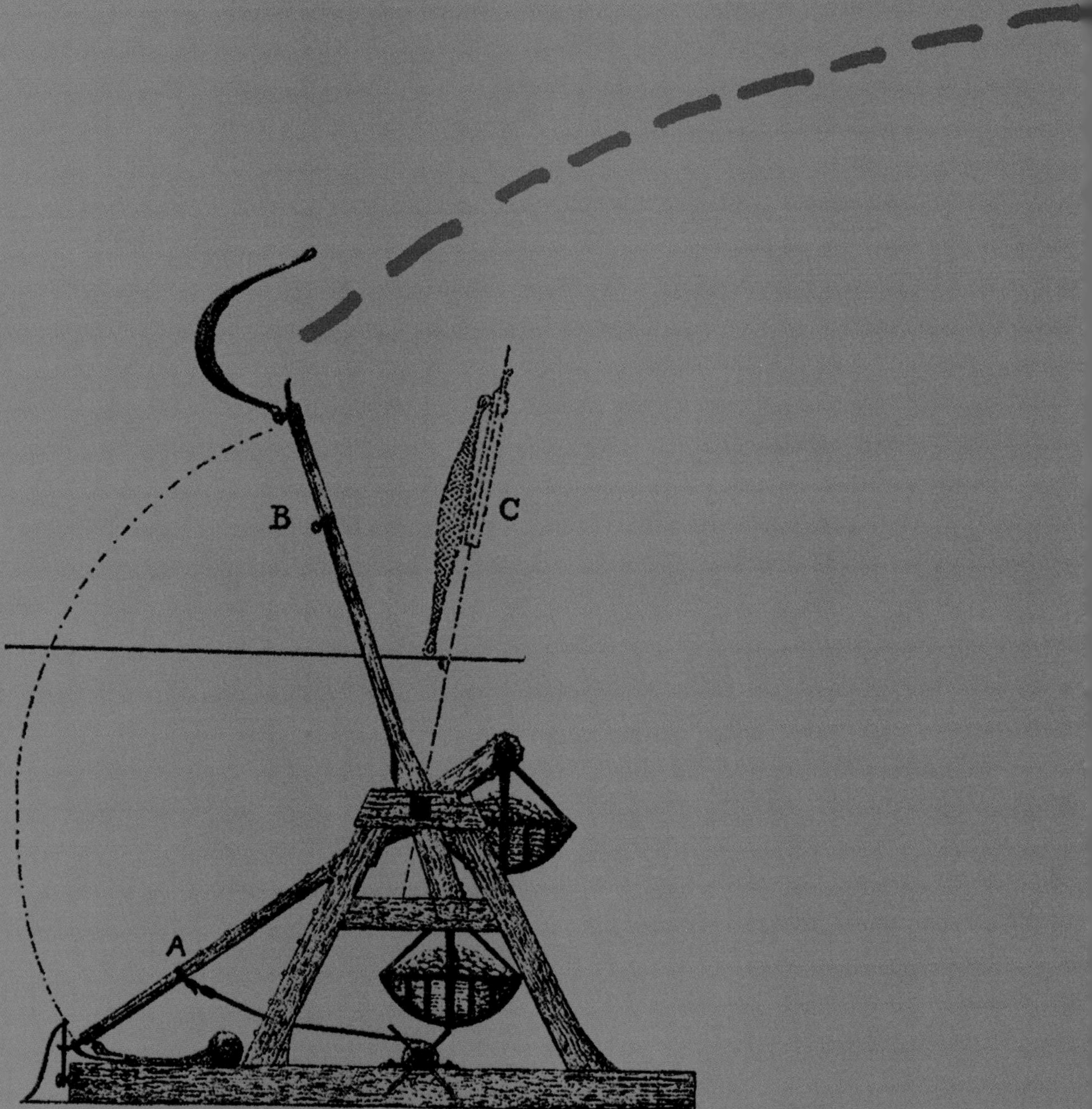

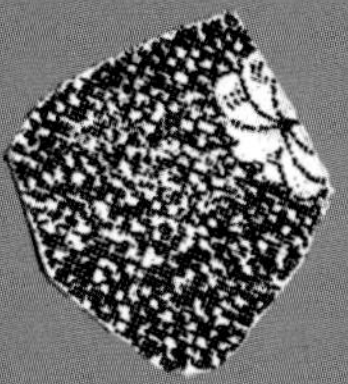

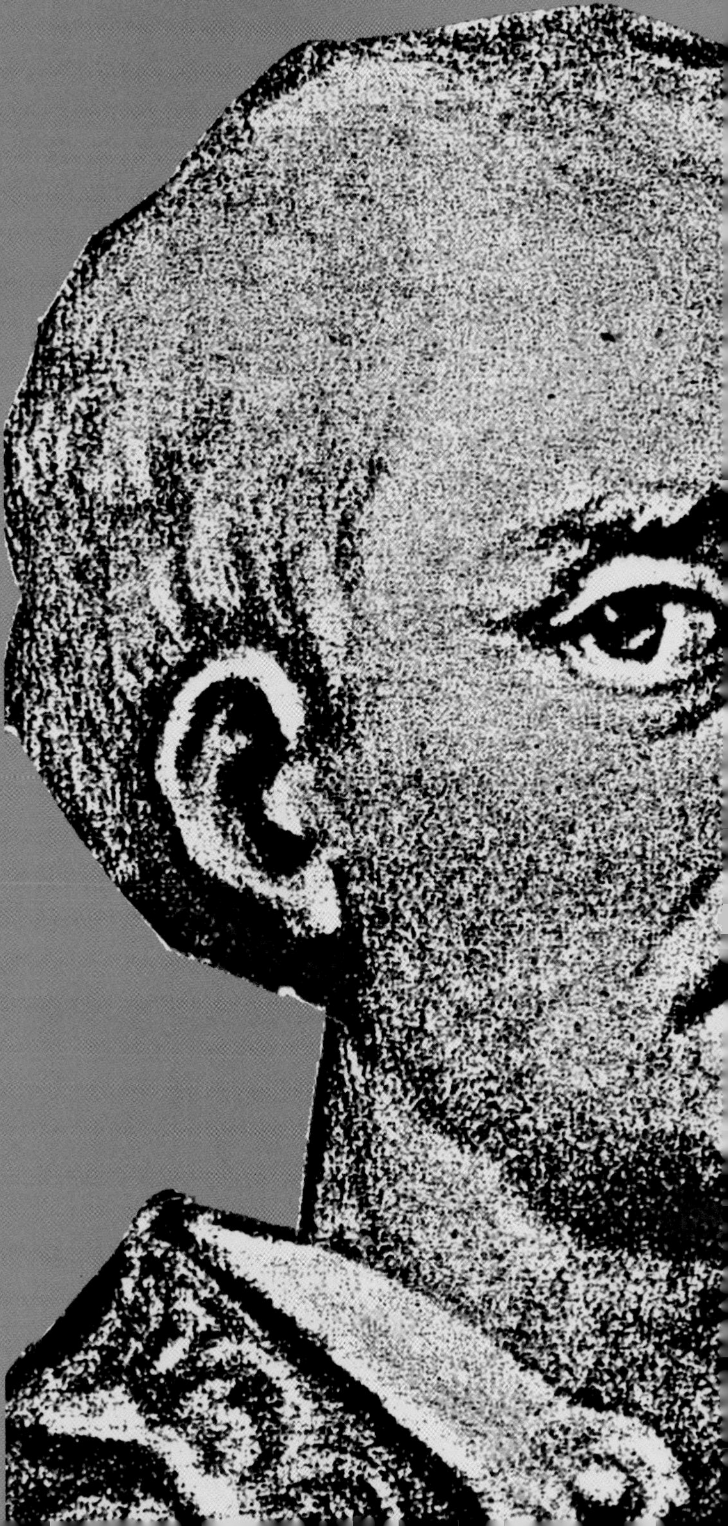

How would you like to die? Tell us all about it.

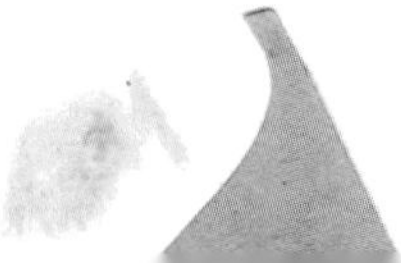

28.

Remember question 27? That was a bummer.

Now, what is your greatest regret?

This page for do-overs.

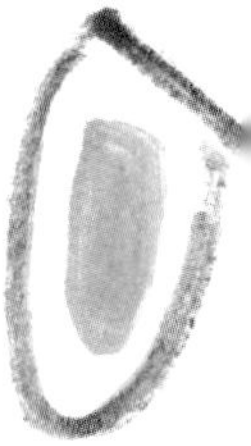

ATTITUDE MEASUREMENT

God, our timing couldn't be worse.

Who or What is the GREATEST LOVE of your Life?

TELL US ALL ABOUT IT.

Pen an ode. (Or heartfelt email.)

30.

Have we covered everything?

What else could you possibly tell us
that we don't already know?

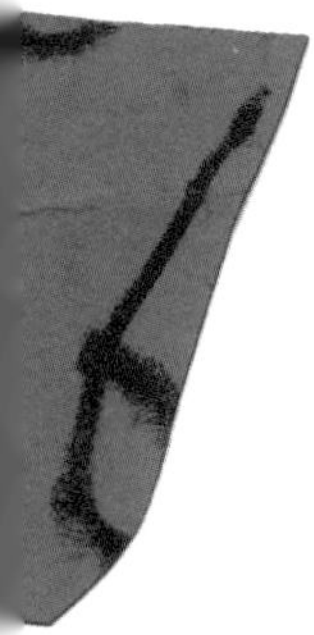

Preferred cousin? Favorite land mass? Relationship to gluten? Truth versus beauty? Dream tattoo?

FIN

Acknowledgments

Thank you to the TarcherPerigee team: John Duff, who dreamed up the project and found me through Canadian birdwatching back channels (somehow, not a joke). Editors Marian Lizzi and Lauren Appleton ironed out the kinks and gently rolled me toward the finish line. Designer Thea Lorentzen is a talent and a joy and tolerated my cascading requests. Molly Kleiman, Caolan Madden, and André da Loba lent me their sharp eyes and good looks. Evan Kindley is hip to questionnaires and hipped me, too (read his book *Questionnaire*). Grandma, Dad, Amanda, Rebecca, Melissa, Joe, Barry, Emil, Alana, and Leo are my family: thanks to them.

Question 23 asks who influenced you more than any other. That's easy. This book is for my mother, who would've bought ten copies and added them to a special display shelf, the one filled with the things her daughters had made.

About the Illustrator

Joanna Neborsky illustrates books and makes animations for people who ask nicely. Proust is her third Frenchman, after Félix Fénéon (*Illustrated Three-Line Novels*, 2010) and Gustave Flaubert (*A Partial Inventory of Gustave Flaubert's Personal Effects*, 2012). She lives in Los Angeles.